Apollo 11: 74 Fascinating Facts For Kids

Rod Weston

This book is just one of a series of "Fascinating Facts For Kids" books. For more fascinating facts about people, history, animals and much more please visit:

www.fascinatingfactsforkids.com

Contents

The Race to the Moon.........................1

Mercury and Gemini......................... 5

The Apollo Spacecraft........................9

The Apollo Program........................... 14

The Astronauts................................... 17

Launch Day... 21

The Journey to the Moon....................26

"The Eagle Has Landed"..................... 28

One Small Step................................... 30

The Journey Home........................... 35

Illustration Attributions....................41

The Race to the Moon

1. The Space Race began following the end of World War 2 when the world's two superpowers, the USA and the Soviet Union, competed with each other to gain control of space and land a man on the Moon.

2. The first success of the Space Race was achieved by the Soviet Union on October 4 1957 when an artificial satellite - Sputnik 1 - was sent into orbit around the Earth.

A replica of Sputnik 1

3. Two month's after the Sputnik launch, America responded with an attempt to send its own satellite into orbit. Millions of Americans watching the launch on live TV saw the rocket carrying the satellite explode as it tried to lift off. It was a humiliating failure for the United States.

The rocket explodes on the launch pad

4. The Soviet Union had more success on April 12 1961 when the Soviet cosmonaut, Yuri Gagarin, became the first human being to reach space. His flight lasted 108 minutes as his Vostok spacecraft flew a complete orbit around the Earth.

5. Three weeks after Gagarin's flight, the
United States responded by sending the first
American, Alan Shepard, into space. His flight
lasted just 15 minutes and didn't reach Earth
orbit, but it proved that America could at last
compete with the Soviet Union.

Alan Shepard in space

6. Alan Shepard's flight convinced the
American president, John F. Kennedy, that the
United States could get to the Moon before the
Soviets. He promised the American space
agency, NASA, all the money it needed to land a
man on the Moon before the end of the decade -
just seven years away. It was a huge challenge for
NASA.

President John F. Kennedy

Mercury and Gemini

7. In 1959 NASA had selected seven military test pilots from hundreds of applicants to train as astronauts on the new "Project Mercury". The "Original Seven", as they were known, were - Scott Carpenter, Gordon Cooper, John Glenn, Gus Grissom, Walter Schirra, Alan Shepard and Deke Slayton.

The Original Seven

8. The aims of Project Mercury were to send a manned spacecraft into orbit around the Earth and to get it back safely, and also to see whether human beings were able to survive in the harsh environment of space.

9. The goal of sending a man into orbit was achieved on February 20 1962 when John Glenn became the first American to orbit the Earth. His five-hour mission was a complete success and the race to the Moon was on.

John Glenn

10. Project Mercury saw six men sent into space between 1961 and 1963, before being replaced by the even more ambitious "Project Gemini".

11. Each Gemini spacecraft carried two astronauts and they spent up to two weeks in orbit testing a man's ability to fly for long periods in space.

12. Gemini 4, the second manned Gemini mission, saw Ed White become the first American astronaut to perform a spacewalk. The 20 minutes he spent floating in space proved that a spacesuit could keep a man alive outside his spacecraft - which would need to happen when a man walked on the Moon.

Ed White during his spacewalk

13. As well as testing an astronaut's ability to live and work for long periods in space, Gemini was also used to practice and perfect the rendezvous and docking of spacecraft - which would be needed on a mission to the Moon.

14. Mercury and Gemini were both great successes and proved that it should be possible to send a man to the Moon and return him safely to Earth. The Gemini missions were followed by the "Apollo Program", which would carry out even more testing and preparation in order to send a man on the long journey to the Moon.

The Apollo Spacecraft

15. Three spacecraft were needed for a mission to land men on the Moon. A massive, powerful rocket would blast off into orbit above the Earth. It would carry three astronauts and two other smaller spacecraft.

16. Attached to the top of the giant rocket would be the second spacecraft - the Command/Service Module. The third spacecraft - the Lunar Module - would be packed in tightly behind and pulled free and joined on to the Command/Service Module when in space. It would be the Lunar Module that would land two astronauts on the Moon.

Saturn V

17. It would need an incredibly fast and powerful rocket to enable a crew of three astronauts and all their equipment to escape the Earth's gravity, so NASA engineers designed and built the biggest, heaviest and most powerful rocket ever built - the Saturn V.

18. The Saturn V rocket stood 363 feet (111 m) tall - as high as a 36-storey building. It was three times taller than the Gemini rockets and four times taller than the rockets used in Project Mercury.

The Saturn V

19. The Saturn V was built in three sections - or "stages" - each filled with massive quantities of rocket fuel. When the fuel was used up in the first two stages, these would separate from the rest of the rocket and fall back to Earth. The third stage would be used to propel the Command/ Service Module towards the Moon, after which it would separate before traveling deeper into space and going into orbit around the Sun.

The Command/Service Module

20. The cone-shaped Command Module was where the astronauts lived and worked during the trip to the Moon, and connected to it was the Service Module which supplied the Command Module with rocket power, oxygen and water.

The Command/Service Module

21. The Command Module was the nerve center of the journey to the Moon and contained the instruments and controls which enabled the astronauts to fly the spacecraft on the right course. It was the only part of the Saturn V which returned to Earth - all the other parts either fell back to Earth, remained in space, or were left on the Moon.

The Lunar Module

22. The Lunar Module was designed specifically for landing on the Moon. As there is no atmosphere on the Moon, the spacecraft didn't need to be streamlined or aerodynamic, and it looked unlike any other rocket ever built. Although it looked flimsy and fragile, it was a fine, robust spacecraft and was said to fly like a "nimble, responsive jet fighter".

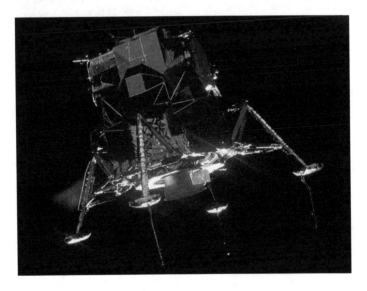

The Lunar Module

23. The Lunar Module was built in two sections. The lower "Descent Stage" included the four long legs which would touch down on the

Moon's surface, the engines to control the descent and the fuel tanks.

24. The top half of the Lunar Module - the "Ascent Stage"- contained the crew's cabin and all the instruments and controls. When the mission was over the Ascent Stage would use its own engine to blast off from the Moon using the Descent Stage as a launch pad.

The Apollo Program

25. The Apollo Program followed the successes of Mercury and Gemini and each manned mission would see a crew of three astronauts being launched into space on board the Saturn V rocket. When the time came to land on the Moon, two of the astronauts would descend to the surface in the Lunar Module while the third astronaut would remain in control of the Command Module in orbit around the Moon.

26. The first mission of the Apollo Program was due for launch in February 1967, but tragedy struck a month earlier when the crew lost their lives during a pre-flight test which went wrong. A fire swept through the Command Module killing astronauts Virgil "Gus" Grissom, Ed White and Roger Chaffee.

Gus Grissom, Ed White & Roger Chaffee

27. The Apollo 1 tragedy saw the Apollo Program pause for nearly a year as lessons were learned and changes made to ensure that nothing like that ever happened again. The Apollo 2 and 3 missions were cancelled and the program started again on November 9 1967 with the launch of Apollo 4.

28. Between January 1968 and May 1969 there were six more Apollo missions. Each mission built on the previous one, testing and perfecting everything needed to pave the way for Apollo 11, the mission which would finally see men walk on the Moon.

29. The main accomplishments of the Apollo missions before the launch of Apollo 11 were:

Apollo 4 -   The first Saturn V launch (unmanned)
Apollo 5 -   The first Lunar Module mission (unmanned)
Apollo 7 -   The first manned launch of Saturn V
Apollo 8 -   The first humans reach and orbit the Moon
Apollo 9 -   The first manned flight of the Lunar Module
Apollo 10 - The Lunar Module descends to within 9 miles (14.5 km) of the Moon's surface

The Earth seen from Apollo 8 during lunar orbit

The Astronauts

30. Each Apollo mission had used a different crew and in January 1969 the names of the three astronauts who would be the crew for Apollo 11 were announced. They would be Neil Armstrong, Edwin "Buzz" Aldrin and Michael Collins.

Neil Armstrong

31. Neil Armstrong would be the Mission Commander. A former U. S. Navy pilot, he became an astronaut in 1962 and was Commander of the Gemini 8 mission in 1966. As

Mission Commander of Apollo 11, he would become the first man ever to set foot on the Moon.

Buzz Aldrin

32. Buzz Aldrin was a U. S. Air Force pilot during the Korean War and became an astronaut in 1963. He piloted Gemini 12 in 1966 when he set the record for spacewalks, spending a total of five-and-a-half hours outside his spacecraft. He would become the second man to walk on the Moon.

Michael Collins

33. Michael Collins had been a test pilot in the U. S. Air Force. He joined NASA in 1963 and was part of the Gemini 10 mission in 1966, making two spacewalks. Collins would be Command Module Pilot and remain in lunar orbit while Armstrong and Aldrin walked on the Moon. His secret fear was that the Lunar Module's engine would fail to ignite when blasting off from the Moon, leaving Armstrong and Aldrin stranded.

Launch Day

34. The launch of Apollo 11 was set for the morning of Wednesday 16 July 1969 from NASA's launch complex at Cape Canaveral, Florida, where the Saturn V rocket was full of rocket fuel and waiting to blast off into space.

35. Four-and-a-half hours before lift-off, Armstrong, Aldrin and Collins had breakfast together before having a final medical check and being helped into the bulky spacesuits they would wear during the launch.

The pre-launch breakfast

36. At 6.30 am, three hours before the launch, the astronauts were driven to the launch pad where the Saturn V stood attached to the launch tower An elevator took the three men to the top of the launch tower from where they could enter the spacecraft.

37. At 6.45 am Neil Armstrong took his seat in the Command Module, followed by Collins and Aldrin. They carried out checks and procedures to make sure every part of the spacecraft was in order and ready for launch.

38. Shortly before 9.30 am the final countdown began and the Saturn V engines burst into life. When they were at full power the rocket was released from the launch tower and rose into the air on a massive column of smoke and flames.

The launch of Apollo 11

39. The Saturn V accelerated to a tremendous speed - after just two-and-a-half minutes it was moving at more than 6,000 mph (9,650 kph), pushing the astronauts back into their seats and making them feel four times heavier than normal.

40. The rocket had been lifted into the air by the first stage and when its fuel was used up, at an altitude of around 42 miles (68 km), it was discarded and fell back to Earth. Stage two then took over, burning for around six minutes to take the rocket 114 miles (180 km) above the Earth. The speed reached 15,000 mph (24,150 kph) before the second stage was discarded.

Apollo 11 at an altitude of 39 miles, photographed from a U. S. Air Force aircraft

41. The third stage burned for two minutes and took Apollo 11 into orbit, just 12 minutes after lift-off. The engine then shut down and as they orbited the Earth the crew carried out checks to make sure the spacecraft was ready to break free of Earth's gravity and head for the Moon.

42. After one-and-a-half orbits the engine of the third stage was fired again. It burned for more than six minutes, providing "Trans-Lunar Injection" which increased the speed to 24,000 mph (38,600 kph), pushing the spacecraft out of Earth's orbit.

Earth seen from Apollo 11 just after
Trans-Lunar Injection

43. At just over three hours into the mission the third stage was released and the Command/Service Module was traveling under its own power. The third stage still contained the Lunar Module which needed to be attached to the Command Module.

44. Four panels had opened in the third stage where the Lunar Module was stored. Collins, the Command Module Pilot, turned his spaceship around and headed to the Lunar Module where he could dock the two spacecraft. With the Lunar Module securely attached to the front of the Command Module, Collins turned around again and gave his engine a two-second burst which sent Apollo 11 on its journey to the Moon.

The Journey to the Moon

45.   The astronauts spent the three days it took to reach the Moon making sure the spacecraft stayed in good working order, resting and eating. They had been able to take off their heavy spacesuits and wore much more comfortable two-piece nylon jumpsuits.

46.   Enough food and water for the eight-day mission had been packed on board the spaceship. NASA scientists had developed a nutritionally balanced menu of dehydrated and freeze-dried food and the astronauts were able to enjoy meals such as beef stew and chicken soup.

47.   The astronauts were in communication with Mission Control back on Earth for the whole journey. Michael Collins even slept with a small headset taped to his ear in case of emergencies or urgent messages that Mission Control might need to send.

48.   People back on Earth were able to share in some of the astronauts' adventure. The crew made three TV broadcasts during the flight, showing millions of viewers dramatic images of the Earth from thousands of miles away in space.

Earth seen from Apollo 11 on day three of the mission

49. As Apollo 11 got further and further away from the Earth the Moon's gravity pulled the spaceship ever closer. At exactly the right time Collins fired the engine to slow the spacecraft down to a speed which would allow it to enter the Moon's orbit.

50. As they orbited the Moon the astronauts studied its surface, especially the intended landing site on the Sea of Tranquility, chosen because of its smooth, level surface. They then settled down to sleep and prepare themselves for the next day when Armstrong and Aldrin would descend to the Moon's surface.

"The Eagle Has Landed"

51. On the fifth day of the mission, Armstrong and Aldrin crawled down the connecting tunnel from the Command Module into the Lunar Module, which was known as "Eagle". Checks were carried out to make sure the spacecraft was good for undocking.

52. When the astronauts were satisfied, Collins pressed a button in the Command Module which separated the two spacecraft and Eagle floated into space under its own power. Armstrong radioed a message to Mission Control - "The Eagle has wings!"

The Lunar Module after separation

53. Armstrong and Aldrin fired the descent engine and Eagle began its journey towards the

Moon's surface. Collins would be left alone in the Command Module, orbiting the Moon for the next 28 hours.

54. The descent proceeded smoothly apart from a moment of concern when an alarm light flashed on Eagle's instrument panel. Mission Control carried out checks back on Earth and decided that it was a false alarm and that the descent could continue.

55. As the landing site on the Sea of Tranquility came into view Armstrong saw that it was not as flat as had been thought. The area was covered with large boulders and was not a safe place to land. Eagle was just 100 feet (30 m) above the surface and running out of fuel, but Armstrong managed to spot a place which would be suitable for landing.

56. With just seconds of fuel remaining, Armstrong guided Eagle towards the Moon's surface before landing safely in a cloud of dust. His heart rate had doubled to 150 beats per minute, but he calmly radioed back to Mission Control - "Tranquility Base here. The Eagle has landed!"

One Small Step

57.   It was planned that Armstrong and Aldrin would rest for four hours before heading out onto the Moon's surface. But both men were eager to walk on the Moon as soon as possible so instead they had something to eat before beginning the two-hour job of putting their spacesuits on.

58.   By now it was day six of the mission - Monday July 21 - and 109 hours, 24 minutes and 23 seconds after blasting off from Earth, Neil Armstrong backed out of the spacecraft's hatch onto the ladder attached to one of Eagle's legs. When he reached the bottom rung he lowered himself onto the Moon's surface where he spoke the famous words - "That's one small step for a man - one giant leap for mankind".

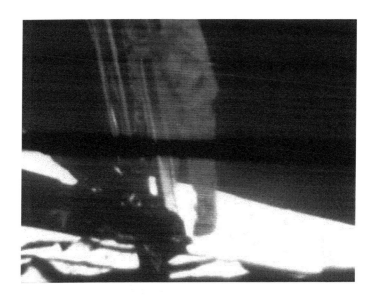

Armstrong descends the ladder

59. Armstrong's first job was to collect pieces of moon rock and soil, so that if there was an emergency and they had to leave in a hurry at least scientists back on Earth would have samples of the Moon to study and analyze.

60. A few minutes later, Aldrin came down the Lunar Module's ladder to join Armstrong on the Moon. They then set up a TV camera so that people back on Earth could watch as they walked on the surface and set up important scientific experiments.

61. A "Laser Ranging Retro Reflector" was set up pointing back towards the Earth. It would pick up laser beams projected from Earth so that scientists could tell the exact distance between the Earth and the Moon. It would be accurate to within 6 inches (15 cm)!

62. A seismometer was set up to measure the strength of any "moonquakes" on the lunar surface. It was such a sensitive instrument that scientists back on Earth could detect the movement of the astronauts' footsteps!

Aldrin stands by the seismometer

63. A foil "flag" was unfurled to catch particles and gases reaching the Moon from the Sun. At the end of the moonwalk it would be rolled up and taken back to Earth for scientists to analyze.

64. Once the experiments were set up, the astronauts also unveiled a plaque attached to one of Eagle's legs. It read - "Here men from the planet Earth first set foot on the Moon, July 1969, AD. We came in peace for all mankind". They also planted a United States flag in the lunar surface and took a telephone call from the American president, Richard Nixon.

Aldrin salutes the U. S. flag

65. After around two-and-a-half hours on the Moon, Armstrong and Aldrin climbed back into the Lunar Module. They had been awake for 20 hours and needed rest before lifting off from the Moon and beginning their journey back to Earth.

The Journey Home

66. When the time came to leave the Moon, many people at Mission Control were worried that the Lunar Module's engine wouldn't work and the astronauts would be stranded for ever, unable to return to Earth. But everything went perfectly as the Ascent Stage separated from the Descent Stage and headed for lunar orbit.

67. After six hours in orbit above the Moon the Lunar Module docked with the Command Module and Armstrong and Aldrin were re-united with Michael Collins. The Lunar Module was separated from the Command Module and drifted away before eventually crashing on the Moon's surface. Collins fired the Command Module's engine for two-and-a-half minutes, accelerating the spacecraft out of lunar orbit to send the three astronauts on their journey back to Earth.

Eagle approaches the Command Module

68. Two-and-a-half days after leaving the
Moon's orbit, Apollo 11 reached the top of the
Earth's atmosphere. The Command Module was
separated from the Service Module and turned
so that the heat shield on its base was facing the
Earth. The friction generated by speeding
through the atmosphere would generate a
temperature of around 5,000°F (2,760°C) and
the heat shield would prevent the spaceship from
burning up.

69. The Command Module hurtled towards the Earth at over 20,000 mph (32,000 kph) - out of radio contact with Mission Control. Minutes later, at an altitude of 24,000 feet, two parachutes opened to slow the spacecraft down to a speed of around 120 mph (190 kph) before the three main parachutes opened at 10,000 feet. The Command Module was now traveling at just over 20 mph and splashed down gently into the Pacific Ocean.

70. Minutes after splashdown the hatch of the Command Module was opened by Navy frogmen and the astronauts were winched into a helicopter and taken to the recovery ship, USS Hornet.

Navy frogmen reach the Command Module

71. As soon as they landed on USS Hornet Armstrong, Aldrin and Collins were put in a quarantine facility to keep them out of contact with other people. Scientists were afraid that the astronauts could have brought dangerous organisms and bacteria back from the Moon.

The astronauts in quarantine being congratulated by President Richard Nixon

72. Armstrong, Aldrin and Collins spent three weeks in quarantine where they underwent medical tests and checks. They were also able to give NASA scientists and officials all the details of their mission. They were finally released from quarantine on August 10 1969.

73. The astronauts were heroes to millions of people from every part of the planet and they spent the next two months traveling the world, riding in parades, meeting world leaders, appearing on TV and telling the story of their adventure.

A parade through New York City

74. Between 1969 and 1972 five more Apollo missions would go to the Moon and ten more men would walk on its surface - but there would never be another mission quite like Apollo 11.

For more in the Fascinating Facts For Kids series, please visit:

www.fascinatingfactsforkids.com

Illustration Attributions

Cover: Title page : Alan Shepard in space :
President John F. Kennedy : The Original
Seven : John Glenn : Ed White during his
spacewalk : The Saturn V : The
Command/Service Module : The Lunar
Module : The Earth seen from Apollo 8
during lunar orbit : Neil Armstrong : Buzz
Aldrin : Michael Collins : The pre-launch
breakfast : The launch of Apollo 11 : Earth
seen from Apollo 11 just after Trans-
Lunar Injection : Earth seen from Apollo
11 on day three of the mission : The Lunar
Module after separation : Armstrong
descends the ladder : Eagle approaches
the Command Module : Navy frogmen
reach the Command Module : The
astronauts in quarantine being
congratulated by President Richard Nixon
: A parade through New York City : Final
picture
NASA

A replica of Sputnik 1
NSSDC, NASA

The rocket explodes on the launch pad
U. S. Navy / NASA

**Apollo 11 at an altitude of 39 miles,
photographed from a U. S. Air Force
aircraft**
NASA / Apollo 11

Gus Grissom, Ed White and Roger Chaffee
NASA / photographer unknown

Aldrin stands by the seismometer, Aldrin salutes the U. S. flag
NASA / Neil Armstrong

66908954R00026

Made in the USA
Columbia, SC
20 July 2019